CCSS Genre Fiction

M000019273

Essential Question
How can we protect Earth?

by Yolanda Garcia
illustrated by Donald Wu

CHAPTER 1 Hurry Up!

"Hurry, kids! We're running late! Grab your lunches. Let's go!" Mrs. Carter said.

Emma and Kate hurried to finish their cereal. They got their lunches. "Come on, Josh, we're late!" Emma complained.

"I can't find my backpack!" Josh replied.

"Josh! Kate! Emma! Time to go!"
their mother called from the car.

As usual, it was a big rush. Every
morning, their mother or father
had to drive them to school.

Kate and Emma grabbed their
enormous backpacks. Then they
ran out the door. Josh dug
through the piles in his room.
"Where's my backpack?" he said.

Finally he saw it. It was behind
the chair. "Found it!" Josh yelled.

"HURRY!" called their mother, not
so gently this time.

4

Josh ran outside. He got into the car. Then Mom turned onto the road. She talked as she drove.

"Kids, let's go over our afternoon schedule. What activities do you have after school?" Mom asked.

"I have dance class," said Kate.

"I have soccer," said Josh.

"I have art class," said Emma.
Their mother just sighed.

STOP AND CHECK

Why does the family need to hurry?

CHAPTER 2 A Great Idea

That afternoon, Mrs. Carter had to pick up everybody. She drove a great distance. Finally they were home. Then Josh said, "I have an idea!"

Emma and Kate were curious. They wanted to hear Josh's idea.

"In science class, we talked about cars," said Josh. "Many people are all driving at the same time. That's bad for the air we breathe. It's bad for Earth. It uses too much gas."

"I think I know your idea!" said Kate proudly. "We could do a carpool to school."

"Yes!" said Josh. "Mom! Let's talk to our neighbors. We could ask Evan Law and his family to carpool. What do you think?"

"A carpool won't help us get ready in the morning," said Emma.

"No, but suppose Mr. or Mrs. Law is waiting for you. You might move faster!" Mom said. That night the family went to visit their neighbors.

The family told the Laws their plan. The Laws loved the idea! Evan Law and Josh were on the same soccer team. They rarely missed after-school practice. Their parents would take turns picking up the boys.

The Carters visited other neighbors. One family said they would drive to school two days a week. Another family had children in Emma's art class. Someone else had kids in Kate's dance class.

STOP AND CHECK

What was Josh's idea to use less gas?

Finally, they had a schedule. It showed when each family would drive. Mrs. Carter put it on the refrigerator.

Josh said, "Tomorrow, I will tell my science teacher our plan. He will be proud of us! We are being careful with important Earth resources."

Mr. and Mrs. Carter smiled. They thought the children had come up with a wonderful idea.

"I just hope Josh can find his backpack! Then we'll be in great shape!" said Kate.

STOP AND CHECK

Why were Mr. and Mrs. Carter happy?

Respond to Reading

Summarize

Use details to help you summarize *Let's Carpool.*

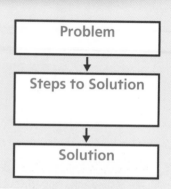

Problem
↓
Steps to Solution
↓
Solution

Text Evidence

1. How do you know *Let's Carpool* is fiction? Genre

2. How is the characters' car problem solved? Problem and Solution

3. Use context clues to figure out the meaning of *know* on page 9. Homophones

4. Write about the carpool schedule problem and how the characters solve it. Write About Reading

Compare Texts
Read how we can keep our air clean.

The Clean Air Campaign

Air Quality Range	Air Quality Conditions
When the air quality is in this range...	...air quality conditions are:
0–50	Good
51–100	Moderate
101–150	Unhealthy for Sensitive Groups
151–200	Unhealthy
201–300	Very Unhealthy
301–500	Dangerous

This chart gives a daily report of the air in your city.

The Clean Air Campaign started in the state of Georgia. It protects one of Earth's most important resources. That resource is the air we breathe.

17

How can we protect the air? Driving less often helps. One idea is to use bikes or scooters to go places. That uses less of the gas supply. It helps keep the air clean.

How Much Energy Transportation Uses

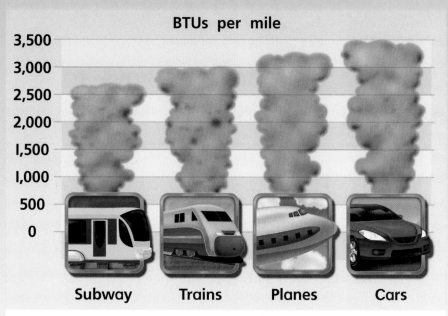

This graph shows the amount of energy (BTU) used by each type of transportation.

In some places, people take a bus or subway to work or school. That also helps keep our air cleaner.

Make Connections

How does carpooling help to protect Earth? Essential Question

What are some ways we can keep our air clean? Text to Text

Focus on
Science

Purpose To find out ways to help the environment

What to Do

Step 1 Think about how you can save Earth.

Step 2 Write down three ways you can save Earth's resources.

Step 3 Draw a picture of each idea. Share your pictures with a partner.

Conclusion Hang up your pictures at home. Ask your family to try your ideas.